Ginny's Gems

Home Management Essentials

*10 ways to make your home schooling
journey simpler and more effective*

by Ginny Seuffert

Copyright © 2010 Seton Home Study School

All rights reserved. No part of this book may be reproduced without written permission of the publisher, except by a reviewer who may quote brief passages in a review.

Printed in the United States of America.

ISBN: 978-1-60704-059-0

Published by Seton Press.
Visit us on the Web at http://www.setonbooks.com/

Seton Press
1350 Progress Drive
Front Royal, VA 22630

Table of Contents

Introduction v

Essential 1: Get Rid of Things 1

Essential 2: Simplify Your Life 5

Essential 3: Simplify the Holidays 10

Essential 4: Avoid the 3 P's 14

Essential 5: Time Management 18

Essential 6: Harness All Available Kid Power 22

Essential 7: Look at What You've Accomplished 26

Essential 8: Implement the Pretty System 32

Essential 9: Take the Pressure Off Dinnertime 37

Essential 10: Don't Give Up 43

Introduction

I may be showing my age here, but it does seem like homemaking is fast becoming a lost art, and the results have not been pretty. I speak to parents all the time who are stressed out about their home schooling, not because of the actual schoolwork, but because household chores are overwhelming them. It is tough to home school when the children can't find their books and pencils in the mess, when babies are crying for Mom's attention, and when it is a thrice daily ordeal to get a meal on the table.

I once had a lively conversation with a thoughtful mom who was considering home education, but had not yet taken the plunge. When I asked her what was holding her back, she told me that modern moms are busier than our mothers of times past and have trouble freeing up the time necessary to do a good job educating their own children. This conversation started me thinking about the time in our country's past when children attended school only a few months of the year—if at all—and home schooling was the norm for many families. These pioneer parents had to haul wood and water, wash their laundry by hand, and in the days before permanent press, spend one day each week ironing it. The items being washed—clothing, curtains and bedding—were sewn by hand. Great grandma and grandpa were spared the task of grocery shopping, which seems to consume huge amounts of time for modern parents. Instead, they grew fruits and vegetables and stored them for the winter; fed, slaughtered and prepared their own meat; churned their butter, and baked their bread. With all our modern appliances and conveniences, it seems incredible that modern parents struggle to keep their homes tidy.

This book began as a series of articles for the monthly newsletter published by Seton Home Study School. Seton parents home school to pass on the Catholic faith to their children and to provide them with a rigorous academic education in a wholesome environment. Seton finds that parents are up to this challenge, especially young moms who in modern times receive an education commensurate with their male counterparts.

Sadly, during this same time, we have failed to educate our daughters, or our sons for that matter, to manage a household. In the final decades of the twentieth century, home economics disappeared from American schools and children filled their time out of school with sports, scouts, and music lessons. Historically, young people learned practical homemaking skills—cooking, childcare, laundry, gardening, and the like—from the older generation. In recent years, the older generation is in the workplace and then in a retirement community in a warm climate. As feminism spread its influence in society, we raised our daughters to be doctors and lawyers, but forget to show them how to scramble an egg.

Intelligent parents with advanced degrees find themselves stressed, not to teach the academic subjects, but to launder the clothing, change diapers, and put dinner on the table. In some families, the struggle is compounded by the regular arrival of a new baby every year or two. The traditional source of household help, Grandma, is, more often than not, working, and Mom finds herself trying to teach multiplication tables in the middle of a mess, holding a crying baby who needs a diaper change.

Catholic home schooling parents do not have hours to sit down and read, so this book is intentionally short and written in plain language. It lays out practical, commonsense rules that anyone can implement, and which can turn the messiest, most unorganized house into a tidy, cheerful home. It is based on my experience as a wife of almost 40 years, a mother of 12 children, and a grandmother of 14 (with 2 more due in 2010). Most of all, this book is based on over 20 years of experience as a Catholic home schooling teacher.

An orderly environment is a tremendous asset for home schooling. Schoolwork goes smoothly when students can find their books and can anticipate a regular schedule. Mom will retain her good humor when she has a plan to keep the chaos under control. Children learn to obey and gain valuable practical life skills. Friends and extended family will admire your peaceful way of life and come to appreciate home education.

Although it is directed to home educators, feel free to pass this little book on to your non-home schooling friends after you have finished with it. These ten simple essentials apply to everyone.

Ginny Seuffert
Oak Park, Illinois
December, 2009

Home Management Essential ... # 1

Get Rid of Things!

Many Catholic moms, especially those who home school, need a quick fix for their messy homes. They do not have the time to read the latest books on the subject, and have even less time to follow the prescriptions these books frequently offer: detailed lists and charts, family conferences, and complicated calendars. These moms need an answer in one line or less, and here it is: **Get rid of things!**

We Americans are drowning in our possessions. The average size of a new single family home in the United States rivals that of the mansions of our grandparent's day. These immense "McMansions" are filled to the rafters with fancy appliances, exercise equipment, electronic goodies, and more toys than any child could ever hope to play with. Added to the equation in teaching homes are books, math manipulatives, desks, chalkboards, microscopes, telescopes, and other educational supplies. Each and every one of these possessions had to be bought, put away, dusted, washed, repaired, and finally replaced. If you never acquire the item to begin with, you do not have to perform any of those tasks. Free up some time. Get rid of things!

Declutter the Kitchen

Here is your assignment, to be completed before you put even one more thing into your home: check out each room in your house to see what you can give away, stow away, or throw away. In the kitchen, keep on the counters only those appliances you use more than once a week. If you bake only for Christmas and Easter, put the stand mixer and the bread machine in a cabinet. Appliances like ice cream makers, coffee grinders, and juicers also should be stowed unless they are used daily. If you only plan on (maybe) someday baking, or juicing, or coffee grinding, or ice-cream making, give those appliances away today. Right now, your main focus is raising your children and home schooling. Do not clutter up your life, or your kitchen, with items that will make you feel guilty by sitting unused.

Pitch the Papers

Pitch all the old newspapers, advertisements, magazine articles, brochures, church bulletins, and home school catalogs you have been saving before someone drops a match and the house goes up like a torch. You probably couldn't find the one article you were saving to reread anyway. Nursing moms, who are home schooling four children and still have two in diapers, have little time for reading and even less time for filing. One of the marvels of our age is the internet search engine, which allows you to access the most current information on any topic. Throw the papers out.

Store precious memories in your heart, not in your home.

Take the family photos, concert programs, and other memorabilia that are spilling out of drawers, and make albums for family members for Christmas. Albums are inexpensive gifts, family members just love to receive them, and the memories are preserved in an orderly way. Here's a solution if you just hate to throw out the old mismatched china, quilts, and table linens you have collected from deceased relatives. Pick a few items you really cherish, and display the rest on your dining table some Sunday. Ask all your relatives over for coffee and cake and invite them to take whatever they like. Advise them you are giving the rest to some charitable organization.

How much clothing does a person really need?

Finally, take a brutal look at your dressers and closets. Will you ever really wear all those clothes? Most folks wear and re-wear the top three garments in the dresser. Get rid of anything that you haven't worn in the last 12 months. Time marches on and so does style; by the time you lose that 15 pounds you gained with the last baby, you'll probably be pregnant again!

Donate those seldom/never worn garments to a thrift shop and let someone who needs them have them.

Getting rid of unnecessary clutter leaves more time to maintain the items you really need. Not worrying about the *things* in your life, allows you more time to concentrate on the *people* in your life. "Do not lay for yourselves treasures upon earth where moth and rust consume, and thieves break in and steal. Rather lay up for yourselves treasures in heaven, where neither moth nor rust consume, and thieves do not break in and steal. For where your treasure is, there also your heart will be." (Matt. 6: 19 –21)

Notes

Home Management Essential ...   # 2

Simplify Your Life!

Home schooling parents who acted on the first Home Management Essential – Get Rid of Things – have a real head start on Essential #2 – Simplify Your Life. Stowing or tossing useless clutter frees parents to concentrate on the real goal of transforming their children into honorable citizens and holy saints. To ensure that our focus remains as orderly as our living space, we need to find straightforward ways to meet our families' basic needs, and not allow ourselves to be distracted by non-essentials.

Simplify Your Schedule

It's easy to wander off track because so many of these distractions are attractive, and appeal to our desire to do what's best for our families, our home schools, our churches, and our country. We want the healthiest meals possible, so we spend hours driving to organic food co-ops and sprouting alfalfa. We want beautiful homes so we try to decorate our houses to look like magazine covers. We spend incredible amounts of time researching the best curriculum choices. We teach CCD and take the Friday evening Latin classes at our parish. We volunteer at food pantries and picket abortion clinics. All of these activities are wholesome and meritorious, but right now, while you are home schooling, you should probably say "no" to many, if not most, of them.

To manage a household, it is essential to spend as much time there--in the house--as possible. Catholic parents with young children, often welcoming a new baby every two years, need to set careful priorities during these irreplaceable early years of the children's lives. **The value of any activity outside the home, no matter how worthy, must be carefully weighed against the time away from spouse and children.** No pro-life work, no parish involvement, no cultural experience will compensate for neglected children. There will always be worthy causes and activities, but your two-year-old will never be a toddler again, and your house can easily spin out of control. Simplify your life by limiting your involvement outside the home.

Simplify Your Household

How time is spent in the home is essential, too. Catholic home schooling Moms should have clean orderly homes, but keep the housekeeping routines straightforward, not overly complicated or time-consuming. Beds with warm cozy quilts over the sheets take only a minute to make up in the morning. Resist the urge to have a luxurious bed with lace-trimmed sheets that must be folded down over a duvet and topped with a dozen carefully placed, color-coordinated pillows.

Join the white towel club! White goes with any décor, and new white towels always match your old white towels.

You can bleach them when the kids get them filthy, and they make terrific dust cloths when they become old and worn. Save the color-coordinated towels for when your children are grown.

I meet home schooling Moms all the time who spend hours grinding grains and baking their own bread because they are concerned about the quality of the typical highly-processed American diet. Simple meals can be nutritious, too. Limit purchases of sugary, fat-laden processed foods by restricting your route within the grocery store to the produce, meat and dairy aisles. Have wholesome goodies, like fruit and cut-up veggies, available for snacks. As much as possible, use only whole-grain breads and cereals. You do not, however, need to grow the grain yourself!

Simplify the Schooling

No article on this topic specifically directed to home schoolers would be complete without a discussion of one of the biggest distractions -- choosing the curriculum for your home school. Too many parents spend scores of hours reading and researching, and then trying to procure textbooks and other educational aids, convinced by the available literature that learning will take place only with a curriculum specifically tailored to each child's needs. Certainly, we should change a program to accommodate each student's learning style, but that does not mean building a customized curriculum for each child. Pick a program (Seton Home Study School has been my favorite for 20 years) and modify it if necessary. Do not spend valuable teaching time trying to reinvent the educational wheel again and again.

In practice, this is simple to accomplish. Your third grade son has ants in his pants and balks at finishing his math drills. In place of endless research to locate a more hands-on learning program, buy some flashcards or do more oral drills using the textbook material as a guide. If your sixth grade girl is a great speller, skip writing the words ten times each in alphabetical order, and give her an oral quiz. If your child needs a greater challenge in science, expand on the lesson plans with trips to zoos and aquariums, or purchase science project videos such as the *Mr. Wizard* series.

Here's a personal anecdote that demonstrates what I mean. One seventh grade daughter was a terrific reader and able to handle Seton's workload and more. Seton sent *The Singing Tree* by Kate Seredy for the first quarter book report. To challenge her, I purchased *The Good Master*, a "prequel" to *The Singing Tree*, which she read first. As my daughter seemed to like the author, and Mom loved the content, *The White Stag* also by Seredy, was under the Christmas tree. None of this required any real time investment or complicated planning on my part, but delivered a nice educational boost.

Take the time to think about the activities you do each day. First, consider if the activity is necessary at all, or if it is something that can be eliminated or postponed until the children are older. Second, look at those necessary activities (cleaning, cooking, shopping, etc.) and ask yourself, "Is this the easiest, simplest way to get the job done? What can I do to streamline the procedure?" Third, consider if you are spending too much time designing and procuring your child's curriculum, and remind yourself that often this time is better spent actually teaching. Finally and most importantly, pray to the Holy Family every day for guidance in how to simplify your life to accomplish the essentials while remaining serene as you go about your daily tasks.

Notes

Home Management Essential ... # 3

Simplify the Holidays!

Home schooling Moms who have read the first two Essentials are hopefully getting some ideas to make their days less stressful. Essential #1 encouraged you to get rid of unnecessary clutter in your home. Essential # 2 extended the meaning of clutter to include those activities which distract us from our primary focus of raising our children in the Faith. By getting rid of things, and simplifying our lives, we take a huge step in the direction of having orderly and cheerful households. This chapter will talk about how we create stress for ourselves by setting unrealistic goals during Advent and Christmas.

I have heard it from Moms often: just when the home schooling seems to be going well, just when the schedule is all set and the kids have buckled down, along come the holidays to throw everything off kilter and once again fill rooms, closets, and hallways with more "stuff."

Do not surrender the victory you won over all the stuff you tossed out by replacing it with more unnecessary

Christmas gifts! Naturally all parents wish to be generous during this joyous season, but choosing gifts carefully will help to prevent us from drowning in a flood of materialism.

First, if dressers and closets are already filled to overflowing, do not buy any clothing as presents. If a family member is claiming to have "nothing to wear," then his or her dresser should be empty, not spilling over! Second, if your children rarely play with the toys they have now, why purchase any more? In both instances, strongly hint that unused clothes or toys would have to be donated, and out of the house, before St. Nick could be persuaded to leave new ones.

Ginny's Gift Suggestions

Consider Christmas gifts that add to family togetherness and fun, rather than to household clutter. Purchase tickets for shows and plays, holiday performances or exhibitions. For older children, give gift certificates for a beauty salon or a favorite restaurant. Pay for a plane ticket for your loved one to visit a close friend or relative. If you want something that can be wrapped and placed under the tree, choose board games the children will play as a group and enjoy with others. Try to avoid expensive electronic games that take up space and isolate an individual child from other family members.

Holiday Entertaining

When it comes to holiday entertaining and other activities, do not forget to keep it simple. Sit-down dinners and buffets involve huge amounts of preparation, so consider some less stressful alternatives. You might invite family and friends to a Sunday after-Mass brunch and serve purchased bagels and muffins, some fancy cream cheeses, coffee and tea.

Parents of large families are often overwhelmed by holiday preparations, but would welcome a social event after the first of the year. You might wish to host an Epiphany Party after the gift-wrap has been thrown out, but the Christmas decorations are still up. Nothing is easier for adults than a wine and cheese party, with a bowl of fresh fruit on the side. If your children want to invite their home school buddies, let them plan their own menu and activities. Guests best remember parties where the hosts are gracious and welcoming, and the conversation is lively. Neither of these requires any work or cost!

Simply be Grateful

The next chapter deals with how a desire to perform perfectly often has the effect of paralyzing us into not performing at all. Watch out for this during the holidays. Here's an example:

Your Aunt Lottie from Cleveland sends you a thoughtful and generous Christmas gift. A thank you phone call could not possibly convey to Aunt Lottie how truly grateful you are, so you decide to write a note. Looking around, you discover that you are out of stationery so you postpone writing the note until you can buy some. The stationery at the grocery store is cheap-looking, so you delay your note writing again until you can stop at the stationery shop one town over. Of course, you are so busy during the Christmas season that you forget all about the paper. Now you are so embarrassed to have postponed acknowledging such a lovely gift that you feel that you should send Auntie some flowers, as soon as your husband gets paid. A month goes by and you still have not thanked Aunt Lottie!

A prompt and appreciative phone call would have been preferable to no thanks at all. If only a note would suffice, you could have torn a piece of paper out of one of the children's spiral notebooks. "Dearest Auntie, This is the only paper I could find in the house, but the moment I opened your generous gift, I just could not wait to write you and say thank you!" Remember: simple is always best.

It will be easier for us to remain serene during the holidays if we remember that, first and foremost, Christmas and New Year's Day (the feast of Mary, the Mother of God) are holy days. The most important decoration in our homes is the Nativity scene, and it takes just minutes to set up. When seasonal anxiety leads to short tempers, I remind my family of one of Blessed Mother Teresa's Christmas meditations. Mother Teresa said we must ask ourselves if St. Joseph were looking for safe shelter for the Blessed Mother and the Holy Child, could we offer them our home? Would the Holy Family enter a house of prayer and Christian charity, or would we be ashamed to have them witness our petty squabbles and selfish attitudes? Your entire home should be a living Nativity scene, focused on the Child born in Bethlehem, and alive with hosannas in thanksgiving for the salvation God has sent His people.

Home Management Essential ... # 4

Avoid the 3 P's!

Faithful readers have received a few simple tips intended to maintain serenity—well at least sanity—as you home school your children and try to keep your house orderly. The best way for home schooling moms and dads to maintain order is through a campaign of simplification. We must simplify our lives by getting rid of unnecessary clutter, and by restricting our activities to those which further our primary goal of raising saints for the kingdom of God. To accomplish this, we should adopt the same goal-oriented attitude that we bring to professional work outside the home. After all, home education, with the purpose of molding great Catholic citizens, is a very important business indeed. Major stumbling blocks to an uncomplicated lifestyle have been identified in the business world as the 3 P's: Perfection, Procrastination, and Paralysis.

Perfection

Many examples of the 3 P's come to mind. Your upstairs bathroom really needs to be cleaned. The sink is encrusted with week-old toothpaste. The ring around the tub looks like a stripe that was painted on, and the grout between the tiles has a sort of green, fuzzy look to it. Three empty cardboard rolls are sitting on the back of the toilet tank. You should get upstairs and clean it, NOW! What's stopping you is that the cabinet under the sink is so loaded with who-knows-what that you can barely shut the door, and it seems to be sending out a funky sort of odor. You can't do the bathroom justice unless you clean that cabinet out as well. That's the first P—Perfection.

Procrastination

You need to set aside an hour, or maybe even several hours, to do the kind of job you know needs to be done. You never seem to find that kind of time, which is hardly surprising as you have four children, three under the age of five, and you're home schooling the kindergartner and second grader. Anyhow, you ordered some very, very effective tile cleaner that was advertised on TV one night at 3:00 A.M., when you were nursing the baby back to sleep. No sense in starting the bathroom before that comes in. Plus, all the towels are frayed, and there is a white sale at Sears, so you may as well wait to clean the bathroom until you have the time to run over and pick some up. That's the second P— Procrastination.

Paralysis

Some time later, the bathroom has hit the critical point. The toothpaste in the sink is now so thick that the drain is clogged. The stripe in the tub seems to have chemically bonded with the porcelain. The green fuzzy haze in the grout has become dense undergrowth, and the children are afraid it will attack them if they take a bath. The door to the cabinet under the sink has broken off from being forced closed so many times, and the base of the toilet looks like… well, let's not even go there! Probably you would be better off if you just replaced the whole bathroom, except you don't have the money for that. That's the third P— Paralysis.

Let's face facts! Things would never have reached this point if you had overcome the first P—Perfection—and kept the bathroom just clean enough. A daily routine of wiping down the sink, tub, and toilet with any spray cleaner that comes to hand would prevent the job from becoming overwhelming. If the bathroom is surface clean all the time, you are more likely to find a few spare moments to tackle the grout or the cabinet, and the clean sinks are less likely to clog. Overcoming the first P helps us to conquer the following two.

Curriculum

We see the three P's on home schooling Internet groups all the time. Little Billy struggled with third grade math last year. He was bored with workbook pages, and resisted memorizing his math facts. Billy's Mom wants to find the perfect math series that will absolutely fit his learning style, and she asks her online buddies for some suggestions. Mom is swamped with suggestions. She should use Seton Math, or Saxon Math. No, no they are too rigid. She should use Math-U-See or buy Montessori materials. No, they are too expensive. She should use ordinary household items and design a math program herself. No, that's too time consuming, she is better off buying a planned curriculum. It goes on, and on, and on. Billy's Mom has spent hours and hours reading these posts or tweets, and researching math programs. She could have better spent the time actually teaching Billy some arithmetic. Daily oral drill, some flash cards, a bit of written work, and spending time with Billy instead of sitting in front of the computer monitor, would do the trick quite nicely.

The three P's can affect even our prayer lives. Some parents with infants and toddlers just cannot find time for daily Mass or an uninterrupted family rosary. Don't allow this to discourage you. Even the busiest families can find a few minutes, here and there, for the Morning Offering, the Angelus, Grace with meals, and an Act of Contrition at bedtime. Teach your children short, but important, pious practices like making the Sign of the Cross when passing a church or uttering a brief aspiration when an ambulance or fire truck races by. As a child, I was taught to silently pray, "Praise His Holy Name," when I heard the Lord's name being taken in vain. We have the habit of starting family car trips with a Memorare and prayer to Our Lady of the Way. You do not need to wait until you can perform every pious activity, just do the best you can.

Let's avoid procrastination and paralysis by setting realistic, if less than perfect, goals. Busy home schooling moms can find only so much time to run their households, teach their children, or pray. By keeping up with the possible, we are more likely to find some time for the desirable. As always, we should turn to Our Lady for guidance in keeping our homes cheerful Christian households.

Home Management Essential ... # 5

Find What Time You Have and Use the Time You Find!

Catholic home schooling Moms and Dads enjoy lives of great plenty—plenty of bills, plenty of dirty diapers, plenty of math lessons to be graded, and plenty of prayers just to make it through the day. The one thing we seem constantly short of is time. Most of us want to maintain orderly households, filled with cheerful Christian charity, but too many of us just cannot seem to find enough hours in the day. The key to maintaining order—and sanity—is to figure out what time you have, and then use that time as wisely as you can.

Even Moms with very young children can pick up a few minutes here and there. One tip is to get up an hour earlier (okay, thirty minutes if the baby was up twice last night!), so that you can snatch a few seconds to straighten up before your husband leaves for work. If the baby is napping, have your school-age children sit at the kitchen table while you do the dishes and get a head start on tonight's dinner. Often an older toddler can supervise a younger one ("Call Mommy if the baby needs me"), while you race down to the basement and throw a load of wash in the machine. The key is to put the time you find to good use.

Stay Unplugged

If I could give just one piece of advice to overworked Moms who can't seem to find the minutes to keep things together, it would be: **Stay away from the electronics.** You may be well below the national average if you watch only one "favorite" TV show per day, but most Catholic home schooling families are way above the national average for the number of children we have. Just one hour spent vegging out in front of the tube could be better spent almost anywhere else. Years ago, when I had only five or six kids, I resolved never to "just" watch TV, especially during weekdays. This good habit has served me very well. If you really want to watch a particular program, plan to fold laundry, mend, iron, or exercise during the show so that you don't waste an entire hour. Hop up during commercials to switch the wash to the dryer, or run the trash to the curb, and you can enjoy your program guilt-free.

Computers in general, and online services in particular, are the worst sort of time thieves. No one can vacuum and play spider solitaire at the same time! Home schooling chat rooms and message boards are filled with Moms who spend hours and hours online, all the while complaining that they can't find the time to check over workbook pages or get meals on the table. Unlike the hands-free TV, a computer does not lend itself to multi-tasking. A good resolution might be to stay away from the keyboard until a particular time of day, say 9 P.M. By that time, most of us are too tired to do much around the house anyway, so it's a good time to answer emails or stay in touch with home schooling buddies online.

Emphasize the Essential

While all of us sigh with envy at the beautiful homes we see in advertisements and decorating magazines, they are not realistic goals for most home schooling families, especially those of us just managing to pay our bills. An orderly home and a simple lifestyle will serve the majority of us far better. In the limited time you can devote to household routines, make sure that you take care of the essentials first, and save the less pressing tasks for Dad's day off.

These essential household chores will keep your home tidy and healthy most of the time. As soon as you get dressed each morning, make your bed, and put any soiled clothes in the hamper. At the end of each meal, you (or one of the children) can take ten minutes to load the dishwasher (or wash the dishes and put them in the drain board to air dry) and wipe the counters. If you have another few minutes, try to sweep. Make a point to put away toiletries in the bathroom and wipe the sink, countertop, toilet seat and rim. As I have lots of daughters with long hair, I sometimes dampen a piece of toilet tissue and swipe it across the floor to pick up the hairs. After school hours, make sure the children put away their books and other supplies, and have them pick up any items you find strewn in the living room, dining room, or den.

Now, these chores can be completed during stolen minutes throughout the day that probably do not add up to much more than one hour. I acknowledge that I didn't mention laundry or meals, and your home is far from spotless. You still need to find time to sweep, mop, or vacuum your floors, dust your furniture and disinfect your bathroom tiles. This simple routine of "surface" cleaning will, however, allow you to maintain some semblance of order and, because daily tasks are not piling up, allow you to attack those larger chores on weekends.

Notes

Home Management Essential ... # 6

Harness All Available Kid Power!

Now that we are halfway through the Ten Essentials, I hope that the recommendations—to simplify your lifestyle, get rid of clutter, and make the best use of your time—have helped you to home school in a reasonably clean and orderly environment. Truthfully though, no matter how uncomplicated your family's routines are, a certain amount of work cannot be eliminated. This is especially true in larger Catholic families. Nursing babies, changing diapers, running four loads of laundry every day, and fixing meals for a small army can certainly cut into class time. Before you throw up your hands and enroll the children in school, try sending them to boot camp with Mom as the drill sergeant, and the children as the buck privates. Their missions will be all the necessary household tasks that need to be done to keep your family army going. The rewards for your hard work will be far greater than a clean house. This training will round out the home schooling experience by instilling self-confidence and a habit of hard work.

For the last several decades, popular wisdom has dictated that any whimper of effort from a child must be immediately rewarded so he "feels good" about himself. "Good job breathing, Billy!" "Way to chew your food, Amy!" Some have remarked that providing positive reinforcement for every task, no matter how undemanding, has produced a generation of young people who do not accomplish much, but they feel great about it. In reality, this self-esteem building hasn't really fooled children one bit. They know they are receiving much praise for nothing much, and as they are not given an opportunity to perform challenging tasks, they do not develop the self-confidence they will need as adults. Giving them daily chores to perform, with the satisfaction of a job-well-done as reward, provides them with the bonus of a confident and competent approach to life.

Toddler Tasks

Training your children to help you with household chores is not as tough as it sounds, and is definitely worth the effort. The key is to start early, while the baby is still in the crib if possible. Making the bed in the morning should be as natural to any child as sleeping in it the night before. As soon as a child can walk, he should be encouraged to pick up his toys and put them in a basket or toy box. Even little toddlers can put soiled clothing in the hamper. Preschoolers are generally cooperative, and proud to be able to put utensils and napkins on the dinner table, or sort clean silverware into the drawer. Parents pay a fortune to send their child to Montessori schools where washing tables is part of the curriculum. Save money—provide a bucket of soap and water, and let your child wipe down surfaces at home for free!

Practical Life Skills Curriculum

Teachers in institutional schools score points when they teach their students to bake muffins or hook a rug in class. Add these practical life skills to your own at-home curriculum. In the primary grades, your students should be learning all the housekeeping basics. Each child should be responsible for his or her own bedroom. Four-year-olds can make a simple bed by smoothing sheets and comforters, and tucking folded pajamas under the pillow. At this age, children can learn to fold laundry, starting with towels and washcloths and graduating to apparel, and are now old enough to put folded laundry away in their drawers. Jobs necessitating the use of large muscles—vacuuming, sweeping and raking—are ideal to burn off some of the excess energy primary-age students exhibit.

During the middle school years, your children should be trained, at Mom and Dad's side, in all the skills needed to run a neat and thrifty home. Let them shop for food with you, chop greens for salads while you mix the dressing, and follow a recipe to bake brownies for dessert. Take the time to show middle school age children how safely and properly to clean each room in your house by demonstrating how you mend, dust, mop, scrub the tiles around the tub, and wash dishes. Teach them how to sort wash and operate the washer and dryer. When a child is old enough and mature enough to obey safety instructions, turn over lawn- mowing duties.

Assigning Chores

Some parents rotate chores among the children, assigning kitchen duty on particular nights, or posting a job schedule on the refrigerator. I have found that allowing children to assume long-term responsibilities gives them a proprietary feeling and they take greater pride in a job well done. For example, if your nine-year old loves to bake, put her in charge of desserts. She might really enjoy moving beyond packaged mixes, and looking for simple recipes to add to her repertoire. Accept her requests for ingredients that must be added to the shopping list. It's her job; let her do it.

In our house, one daughter has had the responsibility of keeping the much-used upstairs bathroom clean for the past two or three years. In this case, familiarity had led to a high level of cleanliness! Additionally, because this is "her" room, she scolds anyone who fails to rinse the tub, or put away the toothpaste. When another daughter cleans the kitchen, she is fast to direct late-night snackers to put their dishes in the sink. Children are more cooperative about keeping the house tidy when they feel a sense of ownership.

Training your children in housekeeping has many benefits. Time they spend on household tasks frees you to spend more time on lessons. As children become skillful and competent around the house, they gain confidence and true self-esteem from a job well done. Additionally, performing chores around the house helps your children grow in the virtue of industriousness. Developing habits of hard work will serve them well throughout their lifetimes, and will help them resist one of the sins against the theological virtue of hope—despair.

Industrious men and women do not despair when the going gets tough. They roll up their sleeves and attack their problems. As you can see, your efforts to train your children have a big payback for you and for them. Get busy getting them busy!

Home Management Essential ...

Look At What You Have Accomplished!

Home schooling Moms and Dads all over America have very mixed feelings when spring rolls around. On one hand, we are delighted that March mud is finally turning into green grass and daffodils. The windows are open, the kids can go outside to play after school time, and we no longer spend hours each day stowing coats, scarves, and hats that family members have been strewing all over the living room for the past six months. In our faith life, Lent is over and Christ is risen from the dead. What could be more perfect? Then why are many home schooling parents still blue?

Too many home school parents greet the greening of their gardens with a gloomy realization that, while the school year is three quarters finished, they haven't had the educational success they had hoped for. All the trips to zoos and museums that Mom has been promising when the weather turned nice seem pretty impossible considering how far behind the children are in their studies. You've been envisioning a brisk spring-cleaning and a sparkling house, but just haven't found the time, and don't see how you will ever find the time before the last child goes to college. By the time that happens, you'll probably die of old age! Many home schooling parents feel frustration and a sense of failure this time of year because of what they have not accomplished.

Take a Moment to Consider Your Achievements

To regain a cheery Christian attitude, a good place to start is remembering what you actually did accomplish since the start of this school year. You kept your children in a wholesome Catholic environment. They read stories about authentic family life and biographies of the saints, learned their math facts and how to compute with them, gained a Catholic understanding of our world's history and an appreciation for the role our Faith has played in art. Hopefully, you were able to attend daily Mass at least sometimes, and had family devotions like Grace with meals, the Angelus, and the Rosary. Your children were able to witness first hand, and be inspired by, your sacrifices and your willingness to give up your own time and material comforts for their sakes. Moreover, your children played with their brothers and sisters and forged bonds with one another that will last for a lifetime. Even beyond your front door, your friends, neighbors, and relatives, who doubted the value of home education, have observed and learned to admire your dedication to your children and your perseverance. They've noticed what great kids you have. Seen with clearer eyes, the accomplishments of average home schooling Moms and Dads are indeed impressive.

"Thanks so much," you may say, "but all your kind words haven't told me how to get my children out of high school before their twenty-first birthdays!" Most of us want to have summer vacation, but hesitate to take a break in the schoolwork. After all, if third grade takes fourteen months to complete, what hope can a parent have for high school in under a decade? And if spring-cleaning takes place right before company arrives for Thanksgiving dinner, how can you believe that you will ever have an orderly home?

A Plan of Action

With all this in mind, here are some simple tips to help you beat end-of-year burnout:

- Set your alarm and make sure you start early every school day. Wake up the children, allowing enough time for them to eat breakfast, make their beds, and be sitting down with their books, and on task, at the same time every day. Wear a watch and check it throughout the day to make sure you are staying on schedule.

- Emphasize the essential subjects, like religion, reading, English and math. Especially in the elementary grades, subjects like science and history can be done with Dad or over the weekend.

- Take some time and look over the work the student must complete to finish the grade. Eliminate repetitious review of subjects in which the student does well. If your daughter is a good speller, let her skip writing the words or putting them in alphabetical order. Allow her some time to memorize the words and give her an oral quiz. If your son easily mastered his math concepts this year, let him complete just the odd-numbered problems in his textbook. See what work can be done orally, and see if bright students can "test out" of some of the daily work.

- Allow the children, especially boys, some break time during the school day so they can stretch their legs and burn off some energy. Assign specific tasks, like sweeping the hall or loading the dishwasher, to get them up and moving. Check your watch and give each child a specific time to sit down and hit the books again.

- As the weather warms, many families encourage participation in team sports, or more class trips with home schooling buddies as a chance for the kids to reconnect with their friends and get some healthy exercise. Make sure that the children understand that these activities are available only when a certain amount of daily schoolwork and regular household chores are completed. Understand yourself that these enjoyable outings cannot be so frequent that they interfere with schoolwork or housework.

- Remove the television, the video games, instant messenger service, social networking sites, popular magazines, and other distractions from your pupil's life. Many home schooling students fall behind, not because the work is overwhelming, but because they postpone actually sitting down and doing it.

- Finally, take one day when Dad is available, and see if you can get grandma or a baby sitter to watch the youngest ones. Warn any child old enough to lift a mop not to make any plans, and spend one day spring cleaning. Launder your curtains, dust the webs from the ceiling, and polish even the vertical surfaces of your furniture. A gleaming house, with (newly washed) open windows letting in a fresh breeze will lift everyone's spirits.

For lots of reasons, I have continued schooling over the summer for probably a majority of the years I have been teaching my children. In some families this works because the children learn to see education as an everyday task and don't lose important educational skills through lack of use.

Keep the school day early and short during summertime. This way, the students work when they feel most refreshed, but have time for household chores and recreation. Summer is a good time to teach practical life skills that will benefit the family the whole year round. Teach the children to help with the yard work, or allow older ones to take turns grilling dinner. Set a rule that friends and outside activities are not to be scheduled in the morning. A proper balance of work and play will inculcate responsible habits and help you in your task of raising confident and holy children.

It is no coincidence that many state organizations schedule their home schooling conferences and curriculum fairs at this time of year. These conferences are often the shot in the arm that home schooling parents need to remind them to place their faith in Christ, through the intercession of His Blessed Mother. Remember that a spotless soul is even more uplifting than a gleaming house, so try to get to Confession. With the sacraments, the help found at a good Catholic conference, some clear thinking, and a good dose of practical life skills, we can finish the school year.

Notes

Home Management Essential ... # 8

Implement the Pretty System!

Until the advent of modern appliances and grocery stores the size of football fields, many American homes followed an orderly schedule for housework. After completing the daily routine of making beds, washing dishes and sweeping floors, many moms followed the order Laura Ingalls Wilder remembered in *Little House in the Big Wood*: Wash on Monday, Iron on Tuesday, Mend on Wednesday, Churn on Thursday, Clean on Friday, Bake on Saturday, Rest on Sunday.

Modern Realities

We can clearly see that this old formula does not work in the twenty-first century. Unlike the Ingalls family, most of us wear our clothing only one day now before tossing it into the hamper. Clothes are rotated in and out of the washer and dryer all week, so there is no single laundry day. Several of my acquaintances do not even own irons, as permanent press has made ironing clothes practically obsolete. Although I still mend a bit, I must admit that most garments needing repair are just tossed and replaced. Today, we buy our butter and baked goods at the supermarket. Labor-saving appliances and the year round availability of food and other purchased goods have rendered these tasks obsolete.

Sadly, no accepted order of tasks has replaced the old outdated one. Often young housekeepers live states away from their moms and aunts. Even when they are close by, the older generation of women is frequently in the workplace and not available to teach the younger generation how to manage a cheerful and thrifty household. Scads of books have been written on this subject, but not many address the particular issues facing the large Catholic home schooling family. With no set routine and little guidance, many young homemakers flounder around for years before settling down to a system that works.

After floundering myself for quite some time, I have come up with a "pretty" system: the house is pretty clean; the children are pretty caught up with their schoolwork; my husband is pretty pleased and I am pretty calm. Like our ancestors, I have a daily and a weekly schedule that seem to work just fine.

Before sharing my daily task list, let me recommend the one vital piece of equipment that every home schooling Mom needs—the wristwatch. People are always asking me how I keep my life together. My answer first is Divine Providence, but following close behind is my wristwatch. The only way to meet your goals is to set them in the first place, and every good goal has some sort of time frame attached to it. Throughout the day, check your watch to see if you are keeping up. I hold my life together with this cheap metal band.

A Good Start to the Day

One practice from our pioneer parents deserves to be preserved and that is, "Early to bed and early to rise." Try to get up at least 30 minutes before the children, somewhere around 6:00 or 6:30, but absolutely no later than 7 AM. Those precious few minutes allow you some quiet time for morning prayers, a quick cup of coffee and a glance at the headlines. I often throw my first load of laundry into the washing machine and make my bed at this time. Wake the children up no later than 7:30. Sometimes I prepare a hot breakfast, but even if breakfast is cereal and fruit, they are to eat, make their beds and be on task by 8:00.

Many home schooling families attend an early morning daily Mass, between 8 and 9 AM. This has the advantage of getting all the children out of bed, dressed and out the door at a set time early in the day, and many moms report finding more time to get things accomplished when they follow this routine. If your family attends an 8 AM Mass, I would strongly encourage you to get the children out of bed early enough to eat breakfast before the one-hour fast begins. If you wait until after Mass for breakfast, the children will not start school until about 9:30 and that is just too late, especially after the primary grades.

Daily Routine

We do a solid three and one half hours of schoolwork every morning, when the students are most alert. I allow one short snack break, but otherwise, we remain on task. We normally attend noon Mass, and then finish our lunches by about 1:15 PM. Afternoon school hours are more flexible, but we always finish up at least half an hour—usually a full hour—before anyone can be freed for play or sports. This ensures that Mom doesn't watch the children disappear out the door and leave her with a messy house. Before leaving, the children run errands (post office, dry cleaners, etc.), and straighten up the house. Later Mom cooks, but after dinner, we all clean up, make sure clean laundry has been stowed, and catch up on reading assignments before bedtime. The next day, the routine starts again.

Hopefully, Fridays are short school days and Mom can do her grocery shopping in the afternoon when roads are not as congested as on the weekend. Saturdays, the house gets cleaned from top to bottom—period! When we get an early start, and keep our noses to the grindstone, we can be finished in the early afternoon, but no matter what, we keep working until it is done. When events are planned for Saturday, the house must be cleaned on Friday afternoon. Being rigid about this weekly house cleaning keeps us from living in chaos.

The practice of resting on Sunday has not really changed since the Garden of Eden. For millennia, those of us who believe in the One True God have kept His day holy by worshipping Him and taking a break from our daily routines. Obeying the third commandment, far from being a burden, frees us from workaholic guilt. Absolved from worry about unfinished tasks, we relax and spend time with loved ones.

Until the middle of the last century, municipalities had strict blue laws and most places of business were closed. It was no big deal to shop on other days, and families typically had big dinners together, or went on picnics, later taking drives or playing games. Trust our Blessed Lord to take care of all your needs and accept the gift of the Sabbath. What a great finish to a busy week!

Notes

Home Management Essential ... # 9

Take the pressure off dinnertime!

Stressed out home schooling moms tell me that it is not the actual home schooling that is sapping their strength. It's not the housework, or yard work, or meal preparation. It's not the endless diapers or the energetic toddlers or even driving to extracurricular activities. Not one of these things causes maternal burnout; rather, it is all of these things put together that some days make mom feel that the burden is just too heavy to carry.

The sad fact is that most of us realize that we are not enjoying these precious years of our children's childhood—years we instinctively know will fly by—as much as we wish. We find ourselves becoming so wrapped up in the hundreds of individual tasks it takes to run a home schooling household and transport our children to their various activities that we fail to relish traditional, simple pleasures of everyday life. This seems to be especially true of mealtimes.

In the United States, family dinner is quickly becoming as extinct as the saber-toothed tiger. Far too many Americans, and sadly too many home schooling families, grab fast food on the way home from activities and eat it in the car or, worse yet, in front of the television. This national trend not only contributes to the obesity epidemic, but also fosters other undesirable behaviors. Study after study has indicated that teens who share the evening meal with their family several times each week are far less likely to engage in immoral or unsafe activities. We need to remember this as we plan which, and how many, after-school activities our children really need. The whole family will benefit if siblings spend more time playing together in the yard and if mom can get out from behind the wheel of her minivan.

Being raised in an Italian-American home, I learned at my mother's knees how to whip up a really tasty meal for a couple of dozen people, but I have observed that many young moms were better prepared for college classes than kitchen duty. Today, newly-married women almost always work until the babies start coming, and then they find themselves too overwhelmed with infant care to learn how to cook. They try to follow some recipes, but recipes often seem complicated and call for ingredients that mom has never heard of, much less purchased. They come to believe that good cooks belong to some sort of secret society with a very limited membership. Not true! Anyone can learn how to prepare wholesome and delicious meals every day. Here are some basic principles and menus.

Do not be afraid to substitute ingredients, or leave them out altogether.

My absolute favorite recipe for cornbread/corn muffins calls for buttermilk. Now I ask you, does anyone actually keep a regular stock of buttermilk in the fridge? Planning ahead and stocking up on such a rare ingredient calls for a level of organization that most home schooling moms cannot achieve, so I substitute plain or vanilla yogurt, which I do keep in stock. The cornbread tastes delicious.

Novice cooks frequently do not understand that most recipes will tolerate some tinkering. The result may be slightly different, but so what? Does your recipe call for Asiago cheese? Parmesan or Romano will work just as well. Hesitate to make that casserole because you don't have a bay leaf? Make it without the bay leaf, and no one will notice. You can use dried and powdered spices in place of fresh. Are veal cutlets $14 per pound? Use chicken or turkey breasts, or pork medallions.

Remember, pasta is your mealtime partner.

Pasta is cheap, easy to prepare, and generally husbands and kids love it. Follow package instructions (boil water with a pinch of salt, add pasta, cook to desired tenderness and drain) and top with your favorite sauce. Some of the bottled sauces are okay, although the good ones are a tad pricey. Do you want to make authentic Italian marinara? Finely chop an onion and cook until soft in olive oil, then add some minced garlic (I buy the pre-minced stuff in the bottle) and allow to cook for just a minute or two more, until the garlic is soft but not brown. Add two or three large cans of tomato puree (or crushed tomatoes, or whole tomatoes pureed in the blender). Throw in some Italian spices (basil, parsley, rosemary, oregano or anything else you like) and simmer for 30 minutes or so. Taste the sauce. If it is bitter, add sugar to taste. If you really want to jazz it up, add a pound of browned and drained chopped meat, some left over pork chops, or cooked sausage. Serve the whole thing with grated cheese. It's that quick and easy.

When I was a little girl, Catholics never ate meat on Friday so we had our pasta *aglio olio*. Cook a few tablespoons of minced garlic in olive oil until soft, but not brown. Mix this with a tiny bit of the water you cooked the pasta in, and pour over the pasta. You can add some minced parsley (or red pepper flakes) and grated cheese and most people will salt it. If your palate can't take all that garlic, it is perfectly fine, and quite authentic, to serve your pasta simply topped with butter and grated cheese. A popular topping for pasta in Italy is sage butter, which consists of several sage leaves allowed to steep in melted butter.

All of these sauces can be used with boxed pasta or the fancier stuff you find in the frozen section of the grocery such as ravioli, tortellini and gnocchi. Serve any of them with a side salad and a loaf of crusty bread. Voila! You have dinner in no time.

Easy Pan Roasted Dinners

An easy way to cook root vegetables, such as potatoes, yams, carrots, turnips, parsnips and the like, is to chop them into bite-sized pieces, coat them liberally with oil (olive, canola or corn), sprinkle them with your favorite seasonings, and bake them in a 350º oven until soft (usually 45 minutes to an hour). Sometimes I add a coarsely chopped onion or green pepper, and some meat (chicken, sausage, or pork chops) to the pan. Usually these will bake a little longer, but an hour and a quarter later you have a healthy and complete meal.

Start dinner in the morning.

If your afternoon schedule will just not allow you any food prep time, get a crock pot. Master a few simple stew recipes. Chop everything early in the morning, put it in the slow cooker on "low" and dinner will be ready to dish out in ten hours.

Get the kids involved.

It has been my experience that even children who routinely resist kitchen chores love to help with food preparation. At the end of the school day, have the children prepare a fruit or veggie platter for an afternoon snack. For some reason, when children peel, chop and arrange vegetables on a plate themselves, they are far more likely to eat them, especially if you have a dressing "dip."

Use a portion of the sliced cucumbers, carrot sticks, or cherry tomatoes to get a head start on a side salad for supper. Chop up some lettuce, wash it and let the kids spin it dry. (Kids love spinning salad, and WalMart sells a perfectly fine spinner for a couple of dollars.) When storing salad in the fridge until suppertime, cover it with paper towels (not plastic wrap) which will absorb excess moisture and keep it from getting soggy.

This Christmas, give kiddie cookbooks as gifts. They contain simple recipes, with easy to follow instructions, and stress kitchen safety. Any food prep the children do can be considered education in home economics.

Plan Ahead

Some home schooling moms will take a day over the weekend to prepare several meals and ease the weekday evening rush. This is a good idea, but as you can see, not really necessary. On the other hand, you should occasionally make double recipes when you cook, and freeze or refrigerate one half to serve later on a particularly busy night. I will sometimes take a day to have soups cooking on the stove: chicken soup, beef soup, pea soup and potato soup. At the end of the day, I have no less than four meals for the week.

This chapter is not intended to be a recipe collection, but hopefully a source of advice and encouragement for home schooling parents. Preparing perfectly palatable meals is well within the reach of just about everyone. Cooking is an activity that should be fun for the family and not a source of stress for Mom. Even more important, mealtime should be a relaxing occasion when ideas and experiences can be shared and family relations strengthened. Some of my fondest childhood memories are of time spent with my extended family around the dining room table. Build those memories for your children, too.

Home Management Essential ... # 10

Don't Give Up!

"As for me, I am already being poured out in sacrifice, and the time of my deliverance is at hand. I have fought the good fight, I have finished the course, I have kept the faith. For the rest, there is laid up for me a crown of justice..."

2 Timothy 4:6-8

As the school year draws to an end, many of us are discouraged remembering academic goals we set last fall that somehow were never reached. We think of class trips we planned, but somehow never took. Moms recall messy homes and hurriedly thrown-together meals, and wonder, "Did I neglect my toddlers? Did I ignore my husband?" As friends and relatives ask when we are going to send our children to "real" schools, we question ourselves—for the umpteenth time— about the value of teaching our children at home.

We Catholic home schooling parents must remember that our ultimate goal is not to give our children a rigorous academic education, or even a wholesome alternative to institutional schools, admirable as those objectives may be. Our ultimate goal is to form souls that will eagerly seek to share eternity with God in heaven. This is not the time for Catholic home schooling parents to question ourselves; rather this is the time to reaffirm and strengthen our intentions to stay the course.

"Fine words," you may be thinking, "but my sink is full of dirty dishes, and the kids are behind in their schoolwork. How can I strike a balance between my household responsibilities, paying attention to my husband and younger children, and giving my students the attention they need? I feel like a juggler with no talent!"

Take some time to think about how you home school, and how you can make it more efficient. Consider your household routines. What can you do to simplify them? Are your meals easy to prepare and nutritious? Give some thought to your infants and toddlers. How old will they be when you begin the next school year? Do they have a safe place to play without requiring your constant supervision? Is there any way you and your husband can get away from the children for a few minutes each day?

Here are a few ideas, a sort of home school examination of conscience, to help get your thought processes started.

Am I trying to do too many extra-curricular activities? Do I carefully consider the time and inconvenience of the activities that we have?

Are you going on so many "class trips" or activities that you cannot finish your daily work? If so, cut back to a more manageable number. If the kids are disappointed, perhaps they will dawdle less on schoolwork! Are many of your outings with a local support group? Make sure that the group schedule is convenient for you. There is no reason that you cannot go to the zoo with just your own family.

When my children sign up for lessons or a sports team, I insist that they come to me with a plan before I consent to the activity, or pay for it! How many hours of the week are involved? How expensive is it? How do you plan to get there? Can you walk or can we carpool? If Dad will be doing the driving/coaching, is this activity so worthwhile that I am willing to give up Dad's help at suppertime?

Do I have a realistic schedule that I can follow on most days?

A smart schedule includes an early and regular start time. It consists of predictable intervals of schoolwork, housework, fresh air and exercise. The children know that at 8 AM, for example, they should be sitting with their books open and on task. They know they may take a 15 minute-snack/exercise break at 10 AM, and that lunch starts at noon. Your older students should be able to anticipate uninterrupted time with Mom after lunch while the younger children nap. Your daily schedule does not need to be rigid, but it should be reliable.

Are there any tips to cut down the amount of actual schoolwork?

Moms-in-the-know have figured out some short cuts that lessen the workload without compromising educational benefits. First, if possible, try to place two children in the same grade for some, or all, subjects. Second, (for those using a program) remember that the daily lesson plan is your slave—not your master! If your daughter is a whiz speller, allow her to skip the written exercises and go right to the weekly test. If your son has memorized all his arithmetic facts, let him "test out" of the first couple of chapters in the workbook. Third, allow your students to do some of their work orally, or on a computer.

If you are using a program that offers help, then use the help. You might receive some simple suggestions that can make a big difference in your home schooling.

Do I keep my household routines simple?

Take the summer to get rid of any unnecessary clutter in your home. Give it away or throw it away, but have a few less things to dust, repair or replace. During the vacation, teach each child one household task, and make it a permanent assignment. That's one less thing you need to do. Kids usually love to do food preparation, so teach them how to prepare salad, or even make simple meals on the grill. Each child ten years old and above should be doing his or her own laundry. That's another thing you don't have to do!

Can I get any help?

Home schooling is the equivalent of a full time job in many cases, so don't be ashamed to ask for help. If you can afford domestic help, get it. If not, perhaps you can hire a home school teen to watch your children or do some light housework one or two afternoons a week. Eating out can be expensive for a large family, but how about asking your husband to pick up grocery store rotisserie chickens one night each week? Perhaps your mother, or mother-in-law, would be willing to take the little kids for a walk to the park one morning each week, freeing you to help the older children with schoolwork. Be creative, and come up with some ideas so you can get help.

How about my spouse?

Second only to the love of God, children need parents who are devoted to each other, as well as to their offspring. Moms and Dads need to spend some time away from all of the children, if only for a few hours each week. Take a walk, go for a drive, or get a bite to eat, but plan a "date" with your spouse on a regular basis. Always remember that no matter how many children you have, one day the youngest one will blow you a kiss good-bye and say, "See you Sunday, Mom." Busy as we are, we need to know and love our spouse.

Do I pray?

Home schooling, especially in the large family, is such a huge task, it is virtually impossible without heavenly intervention. While family devotions, such as grace with meals and the family rosary, are important, they do not replace the need for individual time alone in prayer. Get up earlier, or go to bed later if need be, but spend a few moments each day talking to Our Lord, Our Blessed Mother, your Guardian Angel, and your patron saint, and ask for the grace to persevere. If you can attend daily Mass, go. If there is adoration in your parish, go.

Mother Teresa once was asked how she and her sisters could continue working in the worst slums, with the poorest of the poor, year after year after year. Mother replied that it would be impossible to do this unless they recognized Jesus

Christ in the faces of those they served. We, too, must always remember that, just as the Missionaries of Charity are not merely social workers, neither are we mere teachers, or even parents. We are disciples serving our Creator by preparing souls to spend eternity with Him in Heaven. Nothing we ever do will be more important!

Notes